José Silva's
Guide to Effective
DECISION
MAKING
and GOAL
SETTING

José Silva's
Guide to Effective
DECISION
MAKING
and GOAL
SETTING

▰▰▰▰▰▰▰▰▰▰▰▰▰▰▰▰▰▰▰▰▰▰▰▰▰▰▰▰▰▰▰
▰▰▰▰▰▰▰▰▰▰▰▰▰▰▰▰▰▰▰▰▰▰▰▰▰▰▰▰▰

by Ed Bernd Jr.

With contributions by **José Silva**, **Juan Silva**,
and other top **Silva** researchers and instructors.
From the Leaders in Mind Development
and ESP since 1944.

Published 2025 by Silva Books, an imprint of Silva Method UltraMind LLC.
1st Edition published 1983 by the Institute of Psychorientology, Inc.
ebook and Audio book are available from G&D Media.

For more genuine Jose Silva books and products please visit
SilvaMethodUltraMind.com

Edited by David Aretha

Front Cover design by David Rheinhardt of Pyrographx
Interior design by Meghan Day Healey of Story Horse, LLC

Library of Congress Cataloging-in-Publication Data is available upon request

ISBN: 978-1-965725-07-8 (Paperback)
ISBN: 978-1-965725-08-5 (Hardcover)
ISBN: 978-1-965725-09-2 (Paperback Large Print Edition)

ISBN: 978-1-7225-2848-5 (epub)
ISBN: 978-1-7225-5362-3 (Audio book)

10   9   8   7   6   5   4   3   2   1

CONTENTS

INTRODUCTION

Why Have Goals?

When we look forward to getting something we want, life is an exciting, enjoyable adventure. That's why youngsters feel so much excitement and enthusiasm at Christmas and birthdays. They have voiced their requests, have made their wishes known, and anticipate having at least some of those wishes granted.

Adults experience the same thing with the approach of an anticipated event: the big game, that special party, a vacation to a dreamed-of locale. In your imagination, you see the sights, hear the sounds, experience the thrill of having your wishes come true.

Such dreams spur you to action: You finish tasks so your enjoyment of your goal will not be marred by the knowledge that you left something undone. There is energy, generated by anticipation, and that energy needs to be expended. This is a key to all human progress.

How Goals Motivate People

When there is hope of becoming better than you already are, you will move mountains to achieve your dreams.

- Young people put forth monumental effort to make ball teams and cheerleader squads and to achieve prominence in other activities.
- Adults devote countless hours to providing service in the community, to supporting clubs and charities and drives.

One of the most natural cravings in human nature is to be appreciated.

For some people, mobilizing to action seems easy; for others, getting started is about the dreariest task in the world. There are athletes who would never be stars were it not for the driving force of the coaches, who use their own inner motivation to stimulate others to achieve.

Different Strategies Required

Some people have to see their goals clearly outlined before them in order to initiate action toward their accomplishment. Other people are motivated by encouragement and praise—and sometimes by challenges—from friends and loved ones. And all seek that special feeling that comes with success, that feeling that feels so good and that can be obtained in no other way except to attempt and accomplish a goal.

That's what this book is all about: to help you set goals that are meaningful to you, goals that will help:

- spur you to action
- give you energy to achieve more than you are achieving now
- make the achievement of your tasks an invigorating pleasure rather than a dreary chore

You might want to cut out pictures and create a "Treasure Map." You might decide to make motivational tapes to play for yourself. You might choose to involve others in your plans for the encouragement and inspiration they can provide. In this book, you will discover what to do and when, why, and how to do it.

You will learn exactly what goals are, and why most people do not set goals even though they think they do. You will learn how to make that goal motivate you in the way that is the most effective for you.

You will learn to clarify your goals, and even your purpose in life, so that life will have more meaning and be much more rewarding to you.

What This Book Can Help You Do

What are the results of all this? That brings us to the specific goals of this book:

By applying what you learn in this book, you will find that you acquire the things you want in life (picture yourself with the symbols of success).

- You will be known as a person of action, one who gets things done.
- Friends and loved ones will also reap the benefits (imagine people telling you how much they think of you).
- You will have the energy of a motivated doer, and the pleasant sense of satisfaction of a person accustomed to achievement.

You already know most of what you need to know to achieve all of the above. This book, like the strategies for goal setting, will help you focus and direct your knowledge and your energies so that you will achieve the manifestation of your desires more quickly.

Apply the steps that are appropriate for you. Use the motivational tactics that will help you keep your goals clearly in mind. And most importantly, begin this very minute, for there is no other time than right now to get started. You always have to begin in the present to build for yourself a better future.

To begin, simply turn the page and learn how to convert your dreams into goals.

CHAPTER 1

How to Convert Your Dreams into Goals

The Winds of Fate

One ship drives east and another drives west
With the selfsame winds that blow.
'Tis the set of the sails
And not the gales
Which tells us the way to go.

Like the winds of the seas are the ways of fate,
As we voyage along through the life:
'Tis the set of a soul
That decides its goal,
And not the calm or the strife.

BY ELLA WHEELER WILCOX

A dream is real only to the dreamer. To a person outside of the dream, it is only an illusion. To transfer your dreams to the objective (physical) dimension takes action. The first step is to convert that dream into a goal.

We all start with approximately the same raw materials to work with. What we do with the tools and materials we have on hand is up to us. As we have been told many times, the person who starts with the least often ends up doing the most, for that person must work harder and thus learn more and develop more strength and skills just to survive.

There is no big secret to setting your sails the way you want to go, to give direction and meaning to your life, but you must do it properly, in a way that will be effective. So now we will establish some methodology for doing just that, starting with:

Five Steps to Success

In the beginning of her Silva seminars, Wanda Morris of Houston tells participants that it is important to set goals, and she outlines five "Steps to Success."

1. Decide What You Want

It is surprising how many people don't know what they want.

Dr. George DeSau, a Silva research consultant and lecturer, likes to ask people, "If you could have (or do) anything you wanted right now, what would you select?" It is amazing, he says, how few people can answer that question. We will go into more detail on this in Chapter 5.

2. Convert Dreams into Goals; Make Your Thoughts Visible

Write down your goal. This is the first step in transferring it to the objective dimension. Just like dreams in the middle of the night that seem so vivid to you but are nothing more than the memory of a pleasant feeling when you get up in the morning, goals can vanish quickly if they are not put into physical form. So write it down.

It is good to write down your goals, Silva Method Founder José Silva points out, because "sometimes we have a tendency to deviate or forget or not pay attention or not to reinforce. When it is written down, every time you read it you are reinforcing it. You are reminded to think about it.

"When you look at what you have written," Silva continued, "you always look at it in the present, and as soon as you look at it in the present, it is being recorded in the past. You want to record it many times in the past. Every time you go over it in your mind, you are recording it in the past again.

"When writing your goals, write:

"I will be, I am getting to be, I am closer to being, now I am it.

"You establish points of reference, and move forward: I want to be, I will be, I am getting to be, I am there now. At alpha, in the subjective dimension, of course, you already are successful."

AN EXAMPLE OF THIS PLAN IN ACTION

Silva Lecturer Alicia Curtis in Oklahoma City, Oklahoma, demonstrated the power of writing out a simple goal and reviewing it frequently.

She wrote: "I am drawing the right business for me for where I am in my growth, to teach them The Silva Method so they will benefit."

A few weeks later she received a call from a man seeking training for seventeen directors of centers for alcohol and drug rehabilitation in Oklahoma, Texas, Kansas, and Missouri. When the directors finished the training, they were so enthusiastic that they asked that the training be presented to their clients.

3. There Is Power in Pictures

Get a picture of it. Cut a picture out of a catalog, or make a photograph, or draw a picture of your goal. This does several things for you at the same time: It helps you to clarify your goal; it also helps you to create a mental image of it that you can carry around in your memory and visualize (recall what it looks like) as often as you desire. This puts real power in your programming.

4. Use the Alpha Dimension

Program your goal at the alpha brain wave level, in the present or past tense. This is simple for Silva graduates: simply enter your level and use the Mirror of the Mind or the 3-Scenes Technique. If you don't know how to enter the alpha level, you can learn how with the Free Introductory Lessons at the Silva7.com website. You can also find it on YouTube by searcing for: Silva Centering Exercise Ed Bernd Jr.

If you don't know how to enter the alpha level, think of your goal as you go to sleep at night, and again when you first awaken in the morning. Remember to "pray believing you have already received" your goal.

It is always best to do your programming at the alpha level, the child-like brain wave level. You would have to repeat a thousand "affirmations" to get the effect of programming one time at the alpha level ... at the lower frequencies like those where children function. How powerful those levels are.

Wanda Morris gives an example of the power of that early programming when the brain is functioning at such an impressionable state. Suppose a child is told to "Eat everything on your plate and grow up big and strong."

Then in later life, when the plate is bigger and the person is expending much less energy, driving a car instead of running around, the program is still operable: The person cleans the plate . . . and continues to get big . . . until a diet is necessary.

The prevalence and power of this particular program, which most people received, is evident when you look at the size of the "diet industry" in the United States.

WHY PROGRAMMING IS SO POWERFUL AT ALPHA

Children are so impressionable because their brains are functioning at the alpha level naturally; they are more creative and imaginative than they are rational. And they learn very rapidly.

When you as an adult program from that level, between seven and fourteen cycles per second brain frequency, the range where children from seven to fourteen years of age function naturally, then it is as if you had grown up with that program, that attitude.

In other words, when you put a program into your biocomputer brain at that level, it is almost as though you acquired that program many years ago and have been living with it all this time.

John Kennedy grew up knowing he could be president. Maybe you didn't, but you can insert that idea into your biocomputer brain at an earlier point in time from a brain wave frequency point of view and it would have much the same effect as if you had that attitude all this time. Insert the program at seven cycles per second brain frequency and you will receive the effects as though you had been that way from the age of seven. You program with the power of a seven-year-old child's programming.

5. Claim Your Rewards

In the physical dimension, "act as if" you have already achieved the goal. "Play-like," as Wanda Morris puts it. "Pretend" you already have, or you already are, whatever you desire. Claim your reward, even before you see it, just as children "claim" their gifts mentally even before their birthday arrives.

Several years ago, I wanted to be a Silva Mind Control lecturer. I kept telling friends who asked what kind of work I was doing that "I am working in a print shop." Finally, I started telling people that "I am a Silva Mind Control lecturer." Two months later, I quit the print shop and started lecturing full-time. That's the power of claiming it for your own, and pretending it is so.

Later, I learned that if I pretended to be the best lecturer in Silva Mind Control, and pretended that the people in the audience were the top lecturers from around the world who were there to learn what made me so successful, then things went better and participants learned more and had more successes.

After all, what is the difference in pretending ... and in actually being? If I pretend I am the best, and act like the best, and do exactly what the best would do ... then maybe I am the best.

The Decision Is Yours

It is up to you to set the sails on your ship of life, to take hold of the rudder and steer toward the port of your choosing. If you do not do so, you may wind up in a barren land, or merely continue to hear the slap of the waves on the hull of your vessel as you roll along on an endless sea until the end of your days, never tasting the feast that awaits you if you take control of your own destiny. Nobody else can do it for you. The decision is yours.

As Silva Lecturer Neva Davis of Dallas points out, many people are "Gonna-doers." They are "gonna do it tomorrow" or next week or ... whenever. The tools for you to work with are in this book. You have already started this journey. To continue your journey to greater success, just keep on putting one foot in front of the other, and eventually you will cover a thousand miles and more. That's how to build your stepping-stones to success:

Motivate Yourself

Do whatever you must to motivate yourself and remind yourself to keep working toward your goals. Put up signs with inspirational quotations around the house if you need to. Put pictures on a special bulletin board, or in a special book. This is particularly important if you do not create strong mental images (and many people do not until they practice techniques to improve their visualization and imagination). Record inspiring messages for yourself, and listen to them regularly.

I have used all of these techniques . . . successfully. In fact, without these techniques, I would not have accomplished but a fraction of what I have in my life. Visualization (which means recalling what something looks like) has always been difficult for me. On top of that, I am a very lazy person. Constant motivation is absolutely mandatory for me. And I almost always create my own motivation, rather than depending on it from outside of myself.

Read books that are consistent with your goals. Read about people who have achieved similar goals. Study brochures that give details of whatever it is you are programming for. Spend time with people involved in what you are seeking for yourself. Fill your "memory bank" in your bio-computer brain with "deposits" that will build "interest" in your goals.

Determine whether you are best motivated visually, or through the sense of hearing, or by the good feelings you get with success, and then you will know the strongest way to motivate yourself.

People with a clear image of a goal are the people who are the most highly motivated to achieve that goal. So use your imagination, aided every way you can think of, to keep the benefits of that goal vividly before you, and you will have all the energy you need to achieve that goal and much more besides.

In the following chapters we will look at specific strategies for converting your goals to reality, for manifesting them in the physical dimension.

CHAPTER 2

Strategies for Success

The following strategies have been used successfully by literally millions of people in all walks of life. You, too, can use these same strategies to achieve the success you desire. These formulas work, so take them for your own, personalize them, and succeed.

Short-, Medium-, and Long-Range Goals

A Silva graduate from New Orleans, Gary Terrebonne, who was making little money with his plumbing business, followed the instructions of his Silva lecturers, Roy and Maree Proctor, and wrote down short-range, medium-range, and long-range goals. Then he kept his "ticket" in his pocket, and looked at it frequently. At times he stopped his truck to enter the alpha level, and felt the programming he did then was even more effective.

Within a year and a half, he was earning more money than ever before. His family was living in a luxurious $300,000 home he and his family had designed and built on a lot that they had also persistently programmed for against many odds. They live in the suburbs of New Orleans and their daughter attends the school of their choice, as they had planned for a long time.

Gary wrote out his "ticket" when he started the Silva Mind Control Basic Lecture Series. Within three years of his graduation, he had become a millionaire. That was the long-range goal he had written down!

He told the Proctors and several new groups of participants in the Silva program that he owed his success not only to using the Silva techniques to program those results, but to writing down specific short-, medium-, and long-range goals and keeping that paper handy as a frequent reminder to program as he had learned to do with the Silva Mind Control training. "Coincidences" began happening to Gary, and each one reinforced the next programming step.

A Simple Step Gets You Started
on the Road to Success

It is important to get your own piece of paper for writing out your order, Maree Proctor says. This is your indication of your use of the Law of Life: desire, belief, and expectancy. If you are not even enthusiastic enough to get your own piece of paper and write down your goals, you are not as likely to get your results. So, get a piece of paper right now and write down some goals to begin the flow of impressions from mind to brain.

Write down a short-range goal, something within the next month. Make sure it is specific, something you can picture. Keep it believable, something you are likely to attain. It is good to have an early success to bolster your confidence. Next, on the same "order form" . . .

Write down a medium-range goal, something up to six months away. Again, be specific and detailed. You are placing your order, just as though you were ordering from a catalog, so you must specify all details: what color, what size, how many . . . every detail. Next, still using the same order form . . .

Write down a long-range goal, something to attain any time from six months to two years away. The same rules still apply.

While you want to be specific in ordering what you want, at the same time you want to avoid doing this in a way that limits the creative ability of higher intelligence to assist you in reaching your desired end result. You do not need to program every step along the way. We will clarify this in the chapters that follow.

Achieve It in Increments

Depending on the kind of goals you are setting, it is often best to program your goals in increments, short goals that give results rapidly so you can keep your enthusiasm high. Keep in mind your overall goal, but program specific short-range goals that you can believe you can achieve. Let's take a couple of examples and the way José Silva would recommend programming them:

Changing Your Weight

"To set a goal to reduce weight, a person should first study his or her ancestry to determine what kind of family line they have," José Silva explained. "Were there big skeletal bodies in their family? If there are no other big people in their ancestry, then they may want to start reducing to what for them would be normal. Consider metabolism and your family history, and determine what's normal for you.

"Make short goals, so you can see results immediately, when you program to change weight. Then taper off for a while, then program another goal, and keep going on and off, on and off. That is easier, more effective, usually, than doing it all at one time," Silva continued.

"If you want to reduce 100 pounds, it is better if you set a goal and program yourself to reduce twenty-five pounds first, then you can stop and check yourself, to determine whether you are going to gain again. If so, you can set a goal to achieve what you need to."

PRETENDING CAN MAKE IT SO

Pretending, as we mentioned previously, can be a useful tool. Dr. J. W. Hahn, a Silva researcher, consultant, and lecturer for both the Basic and Graduate Seminars, first introduced me to the idea of "pretending." During one of his lectures he recommended that if you want to be a skinny person, then start thinking the way a skinny person thinks, talk like a skinny person talks, eat like a skinny person eats, walk like a skinny person walks, sit down and stand up the way a skinny person does. Act like a skinny person in every way. Claim it for your own. Observe people who are the way you desire to be, watch them and listen to them, and imitate them.

And remember to accept and be thankful for all the benefits you receive, even if they seem small at the time. One pound a week adds up to more than fifty pounds in a year! By the yard it is hard, but by the inch it's a cinch.

Getting a Lot of Money

"It is always best to program big projects in increments," José Silva continued. "Suppose a person wants a lot of money and decides to program to start earning a lot of money. It is better done in small steps. For instance, some people lose their wits; they get spoiled when they get too much of what they are not used to having.

"Some people are destroyed by their first failure, while others are spoiled by their first major success," Silva explained. "So let's have successes in small amounts, leading up to being able to be successful. Sometimes when a person is too successful too rapidly, they go off in all directions, and don't know how to cope with it. We say do not be spoiled by your first success, or destroyed by your first failure."

Some people set goals so high that they cannot attain them. These people become perpetual failures. There are those who always try to achieve perfection. It is much more practical to program for progress, rather than perfection. It is more rewarding. And it is much more successful.

Formula for Faith Explained

José Silva's formula for faith is Desire plus Belief plus Expectancy. You must have all three elements if you are to get what you program for.

Make sure that your goals are consistent with your desire, belief, and expectancy.

Develop Desire

Desire: The more you want something, the more energy you have to achieve it. This is why we sometimes see "miracles" with participants in the Silva Mind Control program. When you have a life-threatening problem, you have a tremendous desire to correct it. If you then have just a little bit of belief and expectancy, you may get miraculous results. All three elements must be present.

Build Belief

Belief: It is important to believe that what you are doing is possible. This is especially important when your desire is not as strong as it is in a life-threatening situation.

Do you believe you deserve what you have established as your goal? If not, if you feel you are unworthy, or will not be able to handle it, or do not deserve it, then read Chapter 6 for specific steps to straighten this out. And program your goal in increments. It is important to believe in yourself as well as to believe in the program you are using to accomplish your goals.

Program for perfection and be grateful for any sign of progress, because you can use any success—no matter how small—to increase your belief that you can succeed. Mr. Silva said that big successes are the result of the small successes that strengthen our belief.

Positive Expectancy Is Essential

You must learn to take it for granted that when you program for something, it belongs to you. Your "order" may not have been delivered yet, but it belongs to you. It is in transit, and will arrive—in the objective dimension—any time now. That is what is meant by "Pray believing you have already received." Or as José Silva says, "Program in the future in a past-tense sense."

At the alpha level, accept that it is already yours (mentally). At the outer conscious level, have a feeling of expectancy, expecting delivery at any time.

In the next chapter, we will help clarify some of these ideas by discussing how to use goal setting in a variety of life situations.

CHAPTER 3

How to Set Goals for All Aspects of Your Life

There may be a thousand reasons for not reaching your goals . . . but not a single excuse.

You can have anything you want to have, do anything you want to do, and be anything you want to be . . . if . . .

. . . If this is what you need to fulfill your purpose in life. If it is lawful and does not harm any other human being. If you establish your goals properly, then take action to manifest them.

Establish goals in those three categories of life:

1. You Can Have What You Want

I want to have _____. Put any of the material things you want into this category. Do you want a car? Be specific: what make, what year, what color, what accessories, and so forth. Remember, the object is to create clear mental pictures. The same with a house, a stereo system, clothes, tools to work with, or anything else you want.

Remember the rules about Desire, Belief, and Expectancy. And remember that even though you have a big long-range goal, it might be more practical to set smaller goals and reach success in increments.

In this category, as in the others, you can set short-range, medium-range, and long-range goals.

2. You Can Do What You Desire

I want to do _____. Into this category, put your career goals, your recreational and travel goals, your social goals, and other similar goals. Anything you would like to experience can go into this category. Write down your goals, then obtain pictures of them, and follow the other rules from Chapter 1 to help you achieve them.

3. Be the Best You Can Be

I want to be _____. Do you want to be popular? Confident? A leader? Relaxed? Do you want people to call on you because they know you are an achiever? Set goals for whatever you want to be.

Remember, you must select goals you can picture, and acquire pictures of your goals first. For now, put down goals in this category, and when you read Chapter 6, you might get ideas for additional goals to set to help you achieve such things as popularity and feelings of self-worth.

When I sat down to map out goals in this manner, I found the procedure very simple. And it was extremely effective. A year later when I got out my list of goals and evaluated them, I had come to within a few dollars of reaching my financial goals (which had seemed almost out of reach at the time), I was doing what I wanted to do, and had achieved several projects I considered important.

One "Failure" Analyzed

The only goal I did not reach was getting a new car. That was a hazy goal for me; I did not, and still do not, desire a new car. I live close enough to the office to walk back and forth to work and I enjoy the exercise. I probably drive less than 100 miles a month. But when I decide I want another car, I am confident I will get exactly what I need very quickly. The moral: desire is part of the formula for faith, a very important part. Without strong desire, you are less likely to succeed.

A Technique to Increase Desire

Juan Silva, Director of Foreign Countries for Silva Mind Control International, Inc., has a simple technique to increase desire: get a piece of paper and write down all the reasons you want something. Then do some creative thinking (for Silva graduates, this means "alpha thinking") to come up with more reasons. Write them down. The more reasons you have—the more people who will benefit—the more desire you have. And the more desire you have, the more quickly you will reach your goals.

Increase Your Chances of Success

Here is a hint to increase your chances of success:

The more people who benefit, the better.

Do you recall what we said about "desire," the first element of faith? The stronger your desire, the more likely you are to succeed.

That is why it is valuable to consider more than just your own personal benefits and also consider the common good.

José Silva covered this in several parts of the course. The first "Beneficial Statement" in the course is:

"My increasing mental faculties are for serving humanity better."

The final statement in the conditioning cycles reminds you that "You will continue to strive (make an extra effort) to take part in constructive and creative activities to make the world a better place to live, so that when we move on we shall have left behind a better world for those who follow."

I asked him about that statement one day: "That's a statement of unselfishness, isn't it?"

"Without that attitude," he replied, "we wouldn't have The Silva Method today."

CHAPTER 4

How to Convert Goals into Plans that Bring Results

Faith without works is dead.
By their works ye shall know them.

Now that we have taken a comprehensive look at the procedure for establishing goals, let's see what we need to do to develop plans that will bring results.

A goal is not a plan. After you set a goal, you need to formulate a plan for achieving it.

Then, of course, you must put that plan into action.

If you do not take action to achieve your goal, then all of your goal-setting effort will be wasted. You cannot even call it good practice, because you are depriving yourself of the opportunity to discover whether you did things properly, selected a proper goal for yourself, and programmed it correctly. Only by testing it can you determine those factors; only then can you use it as a lesson that will have future benefits for you.

The Future Begins Today

The best advice I've heard recently to help create a plan to implement a goal came from an instructor for a Century 21 Real Estate School. "Anybody can set a goal of selling a million dollars worth of real estate," he said. "The thing that is important is to determine what you have to do today to reach that goal . . . and then do it."

That advice has been invaluable to me. When I use all of the appropriate steps and establish a goal, that goal-setting procedure is only a first step in my efforts to achieve my aim.

My next step is to determine intermediate goals along the way. As we said before, "By the inch, it's a cinch." So what are my guideposts? That is a question I must answer. And I answer it in writing. First, I do some "alpha thinking," then I write down my conclusions.

Organize by Putting It in Writing

Writing things out has many more benefits than just serving as a reminder of the goal. It helps get me organized. Silva lecturer Neva Davis is a big proponent of list-making, and I agree completely.

When I make a list of all the various projects I am working on (which at the moment includes not only writing a series of books, but editing the *Mind Control Newsletter*, preparing promotional materials for Silva Mind Control, presenting the Basic Lecture Series in Laredo and elsewhere, editing the newsletter of the Silva International Graduate Association, supervision production of other books and materials for the company, helping my father with a book he is working on, answering both business and personal correspondence, and more), then I do not have to waste any mental energy worrying about whether I might have forgotten to do something.

I do not have any mental energy to waste, so I make lists of things to do. And I find file folders to put notes and messages into to keep them organized project by project.

So a plan to implement your goal definitely involves planning the intermediate steps, and setting a schedule for completing them. By having your projects and activities scheduled, you can put all of your attention and concentration on one project at a time without being concerned that you are neglecting something important; each project has its own time slot, when it will benefit from your full attention.

Make Plans, and Be Sensitive to Guidance

Lest we make things too confusing or begin to sound contradictory here, let me clarify. We do not want to establish so many steps along the way that we shut out the creative genius of higher intelligence and of our own inner conscious levels. So when you are deciding what you have to do today to reach your long-range goal, recognize that you should be flexible enough to incorporate creative ideas, inspired guidance, and even new directions into your project when they are clearly indicated. Use all of the best judgment you have at this time, and at the same time be open to ideas for improvement, ideas to speed your journey along the path.

To figure out what tasks you must perform today, make another list that contains only today's responsibilities, and then carry those out.

How to Make More Sales

Let us look at how that might work. We will use the real estate example, but you figure out how to adapt this example to your own goals.

To sell a million dollars worth of real estate in the next twelve months, you must sell a certain number of houses. From experience, you can determine how many houses you must offer for sale and how many prospects you must show these houses to if you are to reach that goal. Now you see how we are determining various components of that goal: listing houses for sale and showing houses to prospects are two of the components involved. Let us take just one.

Once you determine how many houses you must list so that you can reach your goal, you can determine, through experience (yours or someone else's if you are new in this business), how many homeowners you must call to get that number of listings. Then determine how many days you plan to work during the next year, and you know how many calls you have to make today.

How to Convert Goals into Plans

Once you start implementing your plan—that is, making phone calls—you can adjust it based on your experience. You might have to increase the number of calls to get the listings, or you might get listings more easily than you anticipated and can make fewer calls, using the additional time for some other aspect of your action plan.

Of course, remember to be flexible, and be willing to adjust your goals . . . upwards. If somebody asks you to list their $1.3 million house, list it. When you sell it, raise your goal for the year. Maybe you will establish a new goal that involves calling fewer people—but people with very expensive houses—because you have discovered that you have a special knack for this. Always keep in your consciousness that there might be a better way, and be open to inspired guidance from higher intelligence.

To learn more about how to get guidance from higher intelligence read our new book *Creative Coincidences*. There is information about it in the Appendix.

How to Get a Better Job

You might set a goal to get a better job. What do you need to do to get that better job? If you need more education, for instance, then your action for today might be to call a local educational institution and order a catalog.

How to Find a Mate

Perhaps you want a spouse and a family, and that is your goal. What do you need to do first? Perhaps you need to take steps to go where there are people, so you can start asking friends about various activities in the community. Or you might want to purchase new clothes, which might involve budgeting and saving money for this. Our new book *Creative Coincidences* has specific advice for attracting the right people into your life.

As somebody said a long time ago, plan your work, and work your plan. Do this, and reach your goals. It might be that you can bypass all of these steps, but by taking these steps you are alerting higher intelligence that you are serious about this project, and you will be more likely to get the "miracle" answer than if you just sit around and wait.

In the next chapter, we will review some tactics to ensure that you are setting proper goals for yourself.

CHAPTER 5

Clarifying Your Goals:
You Must Know How to Ask

Dr. George DeSau, who has conducted numerous research projects for Silva Mind Control International, Inc., and who still finds time for both private counseling practice and presenting the basic and advanced Silva programs, has developed numerous strategies for clarifying goals and putting them into proper perspective.

Two Errors People Make

Errors in programming are usually one of two varieties, Dr. DeSau points out. "The first type of error is stating what it is we do not want. It is an amazing revelation to what extremes we go to keep things the way they are. The subjective, not functioning with negatives, generates what we are saying we do not want."

"I have had individuals who have been Silva graduates for years tell me their programming is not working," Dr. DeSau states. "My perception is that programming is lawful and works. If the programming is not being effective, then we need to look at how and what we are programming. What kind of goals are we setting?

"An improper program is: I don't want to be anxious. The proper program, of course, is to perceive oneself as calm, relaxed, and in control in a variety of settings.

"An improper program is: I don't want to be poor. An equally incorrect program is: I want money."

The first, "I don't want to be poor," is incorrect because it works on negation. The second program, "I want money," is of the second type of error—namely, abstract outcome, he explained. A "positive" program would be programming what you do want—money—but specifically.

"This abstract error would include programming for happiness, love, spiritual awareness, respect, or any number of other abstracts. Many of us have clutched at the abstract as desirable without any blueprint for its manifestation in us.

How to Write Specific Goals

"I have found it to be of primary importance to eliminate this second type of programming error by being more specific as to outcome," Dr. DeSau statesexplained. "This requires a discipline of structuring in the following manner:

Clarifying Your Goals

1. What do I want?
2. How will I know when I have it?
3. How will I feel and act?
4. What can I do now to start the manifesting of this outcome?

"Unless I can satisfy those areas, there is little chance of the abstract manifesting."

"I Want Money"

Dr. DeSau likes to put this in practical terms with a real example he encountered when presenting the Silva courses in New York several years ago. In this case, not only was the programming abstract, but the person was programming for a goal she did not really want: money.

During a discussion of goal setting, the lady said she wanted money. Dr. DeSau reached in his pocket and handed her a penny. "I want more money than that," she responded.

He reached in his pocket and got out a nickel for her.

"I want a lot more than that," she said, showing a little frustration.

Dr. DeSau took out his wallet and gave her a $5 bill. "Is that enough?" he asked. "That is a lot more than what I gave you before."

"No," she answered. "I want a lot more than that."

"How much?" the lecturer asked.

"I want $50,000," she said.

Dr. DeSau put his wallet back in his pocket.

"Now we are getting somewhere," he said. "But are you sure that is really the goal you want to program for? Are you just going to take that money and hide it away so you know you have $50,000?"

"Of course not," she said. "I want it to purchase a house."

"Then wouldn't it be wiser to establish as your goal the acquisition of the house?" he asked.

I first heard that story from another lecturer who told it while presenting the Silva Method in Daytona Beach, Florida. A member of that group volunteered something interesting: He said that he knew a widow who wanted to move into another house, one that cost about $50,000. She did not have enough money for the move, but programmed for it anyway.

It turned out that the man who owned the house she wanted collected antique cars. Her late husband had also collected antique cars. They made a deal, and between the equity in her house and the value of the antique cars to the owner of the house she wanted, she got her $50,000 house without raising any money.

Even financial security is not guaranteed by having money. Just ask anybody on social security whose property taxes and utility bills are increasing more rapidly than their income. Set your goal to live the kind of lifestyle you desire, and expect the resources to be there. Of course, remember you have to participate by taking action to materialize your goals.

What Do You Really Want?

There was a young man who set a goal of getting a flashy automobile. He picked out the exact model, the color, all of the accessories, everything. In truth, though, he wanted the car because he thought it would make it easier for him to get dates.

It would have been more appropriate for him to program to meet a girl who was perfect for him, and he for her. He could program himself to be more attractive to the kind of girl he likes. As we all know, some people can get dates even if they drive battered old heaps. Decide what it is you really want.

In the next chapter, we will take a look at a more fundamental type of decision-making and values clarification.

CHAPTER 6

Decision-Making Strategies: Finding Out What Is Best for You

When you have determined your definite chief aim in life, then the process of goal setting is much simpler. For once you know your ultimate destination, the steps—which we identify as short-range and medium-range goals—are usually fairly obvious.

You could select many things as your definite chief aim in life. José Silva's philosophy in this matter is built on very spiritual foundations, the foundations of service that we see in our major religions.

All Your Needs Shall Be Met

When you are correcting problems on this planet and helping to make the world a better place to live, then you have a right to demand everything you need to do your work and live a comfortable life. That is a basic foundation of the philosophy of José Silva and the Silva Method of Self-Mind Control.

The first step is to do the appropriate mental work: enter the subjective dimension, the alpha level, and determine what your purpose in life is. Find out what you are here for, what you are supposed to do with your life. We are not on this planet for a vacation; nor is this intended as a seventy-year coffee break. We must take steps to meet our obligations.

If I am working to correct problems, to improve conditions on Planet Earth, then I will live a prosperous life. If I am not correcting problems, if I am creating problems, then what right do I have to be here? Perhaps I should beg for permission to even stay.

Our obligations continue while we are still alive and still have the breath of life. Even if you have to drag yourself across the ground, you still have the same obligation to do your best to correct the problems on the planet. When you are not here anymore, then you cease to be obligated.

"In the subjective dimension, you determine what your purpose in life is. Then you plan how to go about doing it. Then you transfer it to the physical dimension," José Silva explains.

If You Can Dream It—And Believe It—You Can Do It!

"That is the concept of the man who said, 'Whatever the mind conceives in the mental dimension, and believes enough to transfer to the physical dimension, you will achieve.'

"So the achievement was the transference of that particular thing that was created in the mental world, into the material, physical world," Silva continued.

"And remember, when programming, you do not program just because you want something, but because you need it. You may not always get what you want, but you can get what you need. And that depends on what you are going to need it for. If it is to correct problems, you will probably get it.

"I program to attract whatever we need. I do not program to receive more than what we need, but I sure put emphasis on receiving no less than what we need."

How to Program for Money

"You don't need to ask specifically for $50,000 if that's what you need to pay your bills; just keep your goal in mind, and program for all bills to be paid, or to have the things you need. Program to see your projects completed, and keep in mind what it takes to do it, as though somebody were looking in and wanting to know what you need so they can send it your way, whatever your needs are. If you don't keep it in your mind, there is no way for whoever is trying to help you to know." Silva said.

"As long as you keep yourself centered, and are fulfilling the purpose you were sent here for, you will succeed and be prosperous in all areas of life."

Do You Program Specifically
for a New Car if You Want One?

"Again, the rules of the subjective dimension: you have to think about it first, and set the rules subjectively before they can be materialized," Mr. Silva replied. You need to pass the test spiritually, meaning: is this correct? Then you are going to get materially, physically, what you need. You should justify your needs in all fairness."

Boosting Self-Esteem

Suppose you want to improve your self-esteem, feelings of self-worth, self-confidence. How would you go about setting that kind of goal? In view of the above comments, you might want to consider doing it this way:

Start with the foundation, the very spiritual foundation of your being, and adopt as your goal that you will do all that you can to fulfill your purpose in life, that you will provide service in whatever way you can and thus become a valuable person on this planet.

That does not mean you have to be famous, or do great things. Everyone on this planet has a purpose in life. Your purpose might be to be the best parent you can be for a very special child. Make this your goal, and let it direct and focus all of your actions. Learn how to be a better parent, how to help this child become better prepared to fulfill his or her purpose in life.

Perhaps your purpose in life is to create something new. Or maybe your purpose is to assist someone else. Each of us, every day, has many opportunities to encourage others, to give honest praise and show honest appreciation. These activities, when sincere, provide a much-needed service that, unfortunately, is not as prevalent as it should be.

Do this, keeping in mind all the time that you have a right to be confident about yourself, to love yourself, and this will be so. Growth through service is a concept worth using for guidance throughout your life.

Determining What Is Important

A friend of mine in New Mexico told me an interesting experience he had regarding values clarification. He is a Silva graduate who uses the Silva techniques very effectively. He enjoys being in business for himself, and created what he considered a good business: He was traveling across the country in his motor home, taking orders for special custom-made jewelry. In his spare time, he continued to study and read, learning all he could about how to be more successful and happier.

One night, he was reading a book about determining what you want to do in life, what your purpose and goals should be. One page ended with the suggestion that before turning the page, you should get paper and pencil and write down your chief goals at this point in your life. Chuck did just that. Then he turned the page.

On the next page was this instruction: "Imagine that you have just six months left to live. Now what would your goals be?"

"The first thought I had," Chuck told me, "was that I sure wouldn't be spending several months away from my family, driving a motor home across the country just to make a few dollars."

He took immediate action: He sold the motor home and caught an airplane back to New Mexico the very next day.

Along the same lines, a young man in Orlando, Florida, once suggested that you should live your life as though whatever you are doing right now would be the last act of your life.

As far as your life is concerned, whatever you are doing at any given time is the result of the sum total of all history up to the present moment, he suggested. Personally, I have found that I like the kinds of things I do when I pretend that whatever I decide to do next might be the last act of my life.

Do You Feel that You Deserve It?

Neva Davis, Silva lecturer in the Dallas/Fort Worth, Texas, area, said she encounters many people who do not feel they deserve to have good things. She suggests that they get a large piece of paper, draw a line down the middle, and on one side of the page write "Reasons why I deserve it," and on the other side, "Reasons why I do not deserve it." Then write down all you can in each category.

By using this technique, if your life is out of balance, you will see *where* it's out of balance. What most people find out, though, is that they lead pretty good lives, and are deserving of good things. The action to take is to reinforce the items listed under "Reasons why I deserve it," and for items under the heading "Reasons why I do not deserve it," ask yourself, "What changes would I have to make so I would deserve it?" Then make those changes.

Silva graduates have a wide variety of decision-making techniques to use. And, of course, they can use visualization and imagination with Mirror of the Mind or the 3-Scenes Technique to help manifest their solutions in the physical world. Put these tools to use.

In the next two chapters, we will consider goal setting when other people are involved.

CHAPTER 7

How to Establish Goals Involving Other People

Everyone has free will, just as you do. So how do you establish goals when other people are involved? Where is the dividing line between what you believe is best and their freedom of choice?

Your first strategy is to use your Silva techniques, or any other techniques you might have that you are sure give you correct information, and seek guidance as to what your goals should be. We have a technique for turning projects over to higher intelligence for guidance: the MentalVideo. You can learn it in our book *Creative Coincidences* by Jose Silva and Ed Bernd Jr.

Here are some general guidelines for working with family members and others:

Programming Someone to Marry You

To the question of whether you should set a goal and program for a particular person to marry you, José Silva has this to say:

"You should program first of all to be sure you have the right person. Check that out carefully.

"Then, after you are sure, program that the other person's desires will be compatible with your desires.

"Then be willing to let it happen the way that is best for everybody concerned."

How to Program Your Children

To program your own children, José Silva suggests, "If you know what you are doing, that is, if you have programmed to determine what is best for your child, and you have determined what job skill is needed on this planet and then you work to help your child achieve that skill, this is appropriate, go ahead and program for it.

"Program that your child will like the field that you have determined, and if the child is successful in that field, then he or she will like it even more.

"When you program a child in this manner, they will accept the area you have programmed, but they can also pick up any other area, too. Nobody is going to hold them back. You know they will be experts in one field."

When You Disagree with Someone's Goal

What do you do when a relative or friend, who is grown, is going to make a major decision that you are convinced is wrong?

For instance, suppose one of your children is going to marry somebody and you are certain this is wrong and it will not work out. Should you program them not to marry?

José Silva's approach is this: "Program to let higher levels take over, and may the best thing be done for all concerned. If they need to go through the experience and learn the lessons themselves, then this is what needs to be."

If you see that a loved one or a close friend is heading down a road that you believe will end in disaster, but that person is determined to continue down that road, then you have little choice but to turn it over to higher intelligence, and then give whatever support is appropriate to the person. That's what the MentalVideo technique is for.

If you tell that person they will fail, then when they do fail, they will likely react against you. What you may not be aware of is that they will learn a much-needed lesson in the process, and you may not have any right to deprive them of learning this lesson, or of gaining the secondary benefit involved in the episode.

Support your friends, just as you would want them to support you. Use your Silva techniques to make your opinions known, at least subjectively, turn it all over to higher intelligence, and then continue to be a loving friend.

CHAPTER 8

Avoid Letting Other People Neutralize Your Goals

The purpose of telling other people about your goals is to solicit more energy that you can use to help you achieve those goals, according to Silva instructor Harry McKnight.

Drawing from a deep well of experience he has accumulated by presenting thousands of lectures on The Silva Method to tens of thousands of people since 1969, McKnight offers these suggestions:

Share with Those Who Support You

"If there is someone who is not in harmony with your goals, who will try to discourage you and give you reasons why you cannot achieve the goal, and thus will take energy away from your goal, then do not tell them about it," he said. "Keep it to yourself."

But sometimes you can gain valuable support and vital energy toward the accomplishment of your goals by sharing them with others.

"You will have some goals that you program and your family, let's say, will program with you," he explained.

"You will have other goals that your business associates will program with you. There will be some that people you are associated with in civic activities will program with you. We have those typical spheres in which we function.

"Within those spheres of activity, you will know what to tell to whom within that sphere," McKnight continued. "You don't necessarily let spheres interact with other spheres. People at work may not necessarily know what your family goals are, although in some instances it might be appropriate for them to know.

"Select the people you share your goals with for how much they will support and reinforce your goals."

Critics Can Help You Clarify

Sometimes, though, it can be beneficial for you to seek out critics.

"When you need to clarify your goals, perhaps as part of the decision-making process, you might need feedback that is critical. Not just positively critical, but negatively critical," McKnight said.

"They can help you evaluate your goals, because maybe you are not considering the environment, or maybe you are not considering the effects on other people involved, or maybe you are not considering that that goal you hope to attain may really be a limitation in the long run.

"Distinguish programming support into various types of contributions to you. Some people support you by encouraging you in your goals, while other people support you by helping you to clarify what your goals are and what the consequences might be. Perhaps they can help you see what your goal ought to be."

Challenge Yourself

There have been times that I have withdrawn from negative comments on my goals so that the energy would not be neutralized, and there have been times that I have sought out challenges to my ability to perform. Let me give examples of both.

In 1980 when I discovered how inexpensive it was to print a newspaper, I decided to put out an eight-page tabloid newspaper for Silva graduates in New Mexico, where I was lecturing, instead of the traditional newsletter that most lecturers send to Silva graduates in their community.

The response I got from the first person I mentioned this to was negative, so I just "shut up and put up." That is, I quietly produced the newspaper.

It was an instant hit with local graduates. And it was an even bigger hit with lecturers throughout the United States, many of whom paid me to provide them with material they could use to publish a similar publication in their areas.

Find Out if Your Idea Works

That story goes along with what José Silva says about proving the worth of your ideas—even if they come from some powerful creative alpha thinking—before getting too attached to those ideas. "Do it, and *then* talk about it" is José Silva's way. You must first have the idea in the subjective dimension, then test your idea in the physical dimension. If it works, then sell it to others.

How to Motivate Through Challenge

The opposite example came when I decided, at the age of thirty-five, to enter a weightlifting contest. I had polio as a youngster, and while I recovered from it, it still caused enough of a problem that I was not able to participate in organized athletics, so this was the first sanctioned athletic contest of my life.

I started the Silva Mind Control training just two weeks before the contest, so most of the time that I was training for the weightlifting competition, I did not have the advantages of the programming ability that you learn in the Silva courses. Therefore, I used another technique to give me some energy and incentive to go through with my plans:

I told a lot of people that I was going to enter the contest.

As I expected, the people I told were quite doubtful that I would ever go through with it. They had known me from my beer-drinking days, and were not at all certain a person would change so much.

That put me in a position of either being embarrassed by backing down or else entering the contest.

I experienced a lot of apprehension as the date for the contest approached, so it was a good thing that I found a way to put some pressure on myself. Otherwise, I am certain I would have decided to skip it.

But I have always enjoyed a good challenge, so even though I was very nervous, I did quite well in the contest, and it is one of the more memorable experiences of my life.

Sense of Purpose Strengthened

I also have a story to tell—a humorous story—about someone helping me to clarify a goal, and measure the depth of my dedication to my goal. It was a loan officer at the bank, who is a very intuitive person and has been a tremendous help to me many times. I'd been talking to him about my plan to lease a building to use for presenting my Silva seminars.

There were many advantages: it would be available whenever I wanted it, I could decorate it the way I pleased, and I could set it up and get it ready ahead of time, rather than having to do so the morning the lecture series began, as was often the case when renting meeting rooms in motels.

But Art mentioned one disadvantage that almost caused me to abandon that goal:

"Have you thought about the fact that you are going to have to keep the building clean?" he asked. "Unless you are going to pay a janitorial service, which will increase your monthly costs above what you have projected, you will have to do the cleaning yourself. That includes cleaning the bathrooms, scrubbing the toilets, and all."

Art knew what he was talking about, because for several years, he worked as a vice president of the bank during the day and operated a janitorial service at night, with Art and his wife doing all the work themselves.

My initial reaction was that a Silva Mind Control lecturer, helping people learn how to be highly successful in life, should not spend the night before his lectures working as a janitor. Especially if that lecturer was me! But I quickly rejected that reaction, and decided it was all right for me to clean the bathroom. It proved my dedication to helping people learn how to help themselves with the Silva techniques, I decided.

In fact, I finally convinced myself it was quite noble; after all, if Christ set an example by washing His disciples' feet, then certainly I could scrub toilets for participants in my lectures.

Monitor your own responses to various situations, and determine how you can build energy for accomplishing your goals. Find out which people will support you, who will challenge you, and who will help you clarify your goals in a loving, supportive manner.

In the next chapter, we will answer the question: How long must I wait to get results?

CHAPTER 9

The Time Factor:
When Can You Expect Results?

Oh, Lord, please give me more patience . . . right now!

In our push-button world, we are accustomed to instant results. After all, we can push a button, twist a knob, depress a pedal, or ingest something into the body and get instant meals, instant entertainment, instant transportation, and even instant "relaxation" and altered states of consciousness (although I prefer my relaxation and altered states to be under my control; those chemically induced physiological states extract too high a price). But we do not always obtain instant gratification.

How does the time factor work when seeking goals?

"If I have a deadline, I would program to have it by a certain date," José Silva suggests. "If not, I would not program a specific date, because I might create a problem somewhere else. I would program it to happen 'as soon as possible,' and I would program to get a clue that it is working, so I can be patient."

"Program to get indications along the way that you are on the right track, so you will know that you are programming correctly," Silva explained. "We should get indications that we are programming right, and we should get these indications within three days. Some 'coincidence' should happen that we can understand so we know we are programming the right way."

Your programming, of course, should always be done at the alpha brain wave level, and at an alpha level of mind.

Strong Need (Desire) Brings Results

When you really need speedy results, you can get them. For instance, there was a time I needed an air conditioner, and it seemed I had no way to get it. I had leased a storefront to use for my Silva lectures. In January, when I leased the space, the weather in Central Florida was very nice, and there was no need for air conditioning. That was fortunate, since the air conditioner in the building didn't work.

By May, I needed air conditioning. We got a nice breeze off the cool Atlantic Ocean waters, only a block away, but a breeze at ninety-five degrees is still too hot for comfort!

I had ordered parts for the air conditioner two months before, but they had not arrived. The man who serviced the equipment told me they would not come for at least two more weeks. The parts had to come from out of state, and to top everything off, there was a trucking strike, and no trucks were coming into the state of Florida.

I received that bleak news late Thursday afternoon. My lecture series was set to begin early Saturday morning. About midnight Thursday, while meditating at my alpha level, I began to do some creative thinking about how I could explain our warm lecture hall. After all, I would be explaining to people how to use the Silva techniques to get things done, so I needed a good explanation for not getting the air conditioner repaired.

Suddenly I realized I had not programmed to get the air conditioner repaired. So I quickly visualized the problem, then the solution, and then went on to other projects.

Perfect Programming

Although I did not realize it until later, my state of mind was perfect for programming such an "impossible" project: I had a great need for the air conditioning so my desire was high; I certainly believe in the Silva techniques; and I had at least a little expectancy, because I took time to program for results.

Fortunately, I did not do anything to neutralize what little expectancy I had, because if I had "hoped" for results, I would have neutralized my expectancy and not had the necessary ingredients for faith. Remember, the instruction is to "pray believing you have already received," not to pray hoping you might get it.

The next morning, at 8:30, the phone rang. The air conditioning man identified himself. The next words I said were, "When would you like me to meet you there?"

He stammered that he had the necessary parts. "I figured that's why you were calling," I said. "I can be there in an hour."

"I'll be waiting for you," he replied. And we had air conditioning on Saturday morning when the lecture series began. I never asked how he got the parts so quickly.

Place Your Order, Please

Results do not always come that rapidly for me, of course, because the need is not always that great. Setting goals, and programming them at level, is much like placing an order for something. It will come. It belongs to you. And while you can see the picture of the item that you have ordered (in the catalog or in your mind), you might have to wait just a bit for delivery to your house (manifestation in the physical dimension).

Keep in mind, too, that it might sometimes be best to set goals in increments. That is, program to trim your weight a certain amount, then get used to that weight before you program to reduce some more. You will want to seek your own guidance to determine when to go "all out," and when to program by increments.

Now it is time to put all of the things we have learned into action and set some goals, make some plans, and get some results.

CHAPTER 10

An Action Plan to Achieve Your Goals

A Bag of Tools

*Isn't it strange that princes and kings, And clowns
that caper in sawdust rings, And common people like
you and me Are builders for eternity?*

*Each is given a bag of tools, A shapeless mass, a book
of rules; And each must make—ere life is flown—
A stumbling block, or a stepping stone.*

—R. L. SHARPE

Knowledge does not mean a thing until it is applied. And the
correct application of knowledge is to solve problems, to make
this world a better place to live, for yourself and for others.

That means you must take action on your visions and utilize what you have learned.

If you are ready to take action, to set goals and make plans that will help improve your life, then read on and do what it says.

The First Step to Take

All right, you are reading this paragraph so you have taken the first step. Now go and get a piece of paper and a pencil or pen.

Right now, please.

Get those tools before you read any more.

Remember what Maree Proctor said: If you are not even enthusiastic enough to do this, you are not very likely to get your desired results.

Now draw three lines from top to bottom of your piece of paper, and three lines from side to side, dividing the paper into four parts both horizontally and vertically. This way, you can select long-range, medium-range, and short-range goals in each of three categories:

- what you want to have
- what you want to do
- what you want to be

Now begin writing goals in any of the categories. You might want to start first by writing goals of things you want to have.

Put these items into the proper slot: long range, medium range, or short range. You might want a car, a house, a new job. Do this now.

Now go to another category; for instance, things you want to do. Again, set goals in various time slots. You might want to go on vacation, attend school, acquire a new profession.

And now go to the third category, and set goals in the various time slots for what you want to be. Perhaps you want to be more confident, or you want to be in love, or married. Select what you want now.

It is important to write down goals in all categories. You might have to begin with long-range goals and work back to the more immediate goals. Do not worry too much about them now, for we will go on and clarify things in a moment. After you write down your goals, then continue with the next paragraph.

How to Evaluate Your Goals

Get another piece of paper now and at the top write down one of your major goals.

Now draw a line down the middle of the page, and on the left side, write down all the benefits of acquiring this goal.

On the right side of the page, write down all of the liabilities.

• For instance, how will your life change when you have accomplished this goal?

- What new obligations will you have acquired?
- How will it affect other people?
- Will everyone involved benefit?
- What effect will it have on other members of your family?

Take plenty of time for this "values clarification" exercise.

Remember to make sure that what you have listed as a goal is really the goal you want to program for, not an intermediate step to some other goal. Review Chapter 5 if necessary.

When you have completed this exercise, then continue.

How to Decide What to Do Next

Now get another piece of paper and write your goal at the top of it.

Then make a list of things you must do to reach this goal.

You can start with general things, then become more specific. Ultimately, you will wind up writing down what you need to do today, right now, to move you along the path to the attainment of that goal.

When you have done this, then continue with the next paragraph.

You know now what you need to do today. So . . . get started. Do something. Remember that what you do does not have to be perfect. The most important thing is to get started. You are looking for progress, not perfection.

As long as you have your goal clearly in mind, then you will be able to determine whether your present actions are taking you in the right direction.

If you detect that some activity is not helping you toward your goal, then make adjustments. It is easier to make adjustments when you are slightly off course than it is to overcome inertia and get started from a dead stop.

So get into action . . . right now.

Successful People Fail Frequently

The biggest thing that keeps people from reaching their goals is that they do not start their projects. And the reason they do not begin is that feeling that things must be done perfectly. But nobody accumulates a string of perfect actions.

In fact, Robert Townsend, the man who made the international rental car company Avis a profitable corporation, admitted in his book, *Up the Organization*, that "Two out of every three decisions I made [at Avis] were wrong."

What Townsend and every other successful person knows is that it is easier to correct an incorrect decision than it is to get someplace without making any decisions at all.

Make Life an Adventure

Townsend also adds that if it is not fun, then why do it? Make your life fun; make it an adventure.

Life is a learning experience, so get in there and start moving and shaking: Move the body and shake the tree, because that fruit is not going to fall off all by itself. The movers and shakers will get it first.

If you really want to be a big success in whatever direction you choose to go, then continue to learn all you can, and, of course, put your knowledge into action. There are many techniques in the Silva courses to help you achieve your goals. Use every technique you know when you are striving for success.

Persist, and you will succeed.

Share Your Successes

And do us a favor: Share your successes with us. If you have any questions, and to share your successes, visit us at:

SilvaMethodUltraMind.com

Best wishes. And may your life continue to become Better, Better, and Better.

AN ACTION PLAN

To Have _____

To Do _____

ToBe_____

Date _____

Signature _____

Mark your "Ticket" like this, and set long-range, medium-range, and short-range goals in each category.

Remember to date and sign your "Order Form."

More Silva Books

To be notified when new books are available you can follow these authors at:

amazon.com/author/josesilva

amazon.com/author/edberndjr

Guidance from Higher Intelligence

If you need more clarity and guidance to make sure you are moving in the right direction and doing what is best for everybody concerned then use Jose Silva's newest technique, detailed in our new book Creative Coincidences

For this and other Silva books, home study courses, and more authentic Jose Silva products, visit:

SilvaMethodUltraMind.com

JOSÉ SILVA'S
CHOOSE SUCCESS
MASTER COURSE
UNLEASH YOUR GENIUS MIND
Original Edition
José Silva with **Ed Bernd Jr.**

CREATIVE COINCIDENCES
The Next Phase of Human Evolution
Influence the Coincidences in Your Life
José Silva and Ed Bernd Jr.

Free Your Magnificent MIND
Insights on Success from **JOSÉ SILVA**
WITH JOSÉ SILVA JR. AND ED BERND JR.

Expand Your **Magnificent MIND**
More Insights on Success from **JOSÉ SILVA**
CURATED AND EDITED BY
JOSÉ SILVA JR. AND ED BERND JR.

SILVA ULTRA MIND SYSTEMS
ESP FOR BUSINESS SUCCESS
USE **INTUITION** TO:
• **SOLVE** PROBLEMS
• **CREATE** SOLUTIONS
• **EARN** MORE MONEY
JOSÉ SILVA Jr.
KATHERINE SANDUSKY
ED BERND Jr.

SILVA ULTRA MIND SYSTEMS
PERSUASIVE THOUGHTS
HAVE MORE CONFIDENCE, CHARISMA, & INFLUENCE
JOSÉ SILVA Jr.
KATHERINE SANDUSKY
ED BERND Jr.